VOL
2

ARE YOU SMARTER THAN A 5TH GRADER

TRIVIA
CHALLENGE
Challenge friends and family!

bend⊙n

Published by Bendon, Inc.
Ashland, OH 44805 bendonpub.com 1-888-5-BENDON

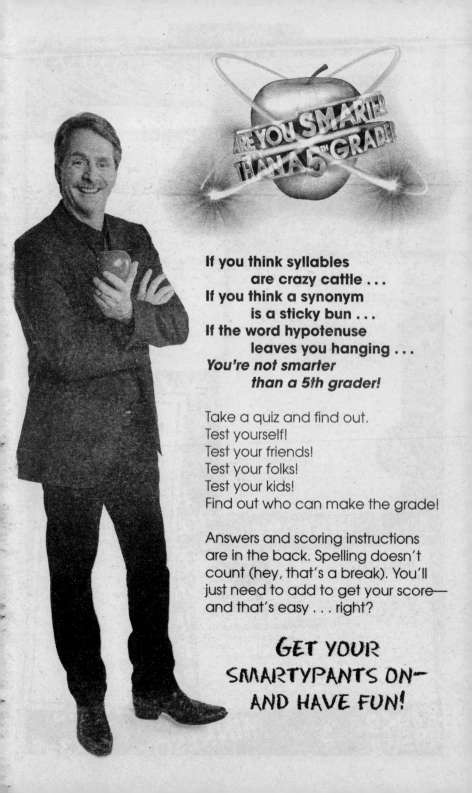

If you think syllables
are crazy cattle . . .
If you think a synonym
is a sticky bun . . .
If the word hypotenuse
leaves you hanging . . .
*You're not smarter
than a 5th grader!*

Take a quiz and find out.
Test yourself!
Test your friends!
Test your folks!
Test your kids!
Find out who can make the grade!

Answers and scoring instructions
are in the back. Spelling doesn't
count (hey, that's a break). You'll
just need to add to get your score—
and that's easy . . . right?

GET YOUR
SMARTYPANTS ON—
AND HAVE FUN!

QUIZ 1

ANATOMY

If Olivia bumps her funny bone, what joint does she hit?

GRADE 1 QUESTION

SCIENCE

True or false?
Neon is a metal.

GRADE 3 QUESTION

CULTURAL STUDIES

What is the official language of Australia?

GRADE 4 QUESTION

MATH

What number is exactly halfway between 1 and 7 on a number line?

GRADE 2 QUESTION

SPELLING

How do you spell the plural form of "phenomenon"?

GRADE 5 QUESTION

GRADE 3 QUESTION

MATH

How many multiples of 8 fall between 14 and 25?

GRADE 5 QUESTION

SCIENCE

What is the most abundant element in the universe?

GRADE 1 QUESTION

ENGLISH

What is missing from this sentence

GRADE 4 QUESTION

ART

Georgia O'Keeffe, renowned painter of flowers and landscapes, was born in what country?

GRADE 2 QUESTION

U.S. STUDIES

The oriole is the official bird of what U.S. state?

MUSIC

True or false? A cello is larger in size than a viola.

GRADE 4 QUESTION

ENGLISH

What is the preposition in:
Man has walked on the moon.

GRADE 5 QUESTION

CULTURAL STUDIES

The Nobel Peace Prize is presented annually in what country?

GRADE 3 QUESTION

ENGLISH

SCIENCE

True or false?
Salt is a mineral.

GRADE 2 QUESTION

ANATOMY

True or false?
The human shoulder is a ball-and-socket joint.

AaBbCcDdEe

QUIZ 4

ART

Which adhesive is usually used for papier-mâché?
A) candle wax
B) paste
C) tape

GRADE 1 QUESTION

U.S. HISTORY

Who was the very first U.S. Secretary of State?

GRADE 4 QUESTION

GEOGRAPHY

What country has the longest border with the U.S.?

GRADE 2 QUESTION

ENGLISH

Which of the following is an acronym?
A) scuba
B) biannually
C) lemon-lime

GRADE 3 QUESTION

SCIENCE

What geologic era are we in right now?

GRADE 5 QUESTION

QUIZ 5

GRADE QUESTION 1

ANIMAL SCIENCE

What is the heaviest land animal?

GRADE QUESTION 5

GEOGRAPHY

What is the capital of Sweden?

GRADE QUESTION 2

MATH

How many sides does a rhombus have?

GRADE QUESTION 3

MEASUREMENT

How many decades are in two millennia?

GRADE QUESTION 4

U.S. HISTORY

Who was the first U.S. President to be impeached?

QUIZ 6

GEOGRAPHY

What is the only continent that is also a country?

GRADE QUESTION 1

LITERATURE

Who wrote the book *Little House on the Prairie*?

GRADE QUESTION 4

U.S. HISTORY

True or false? Benjamin Franklin served as a senator from Pennsylvania.

ASTRONOMY

True or false? The planet Jupiter has a larger mass than Earth.

GRADE QUESTION 3

ANATOMY

How many incisors are there in a typical adult human mouth?

GRADE QUESTION 5

GRADE QUESTION 2

GRADE 3 QUESTION

GEOGRAPHY

What ocean covers the North Pole?

MATH

True or false?
The only factors of 9 are 1 and 9.

GRADE 4 QUESTION

MEASUREMENT

How many months of the year have 31 days?

GRADE 2 QUESTION

P.E.

One might spike the ball in which sport:
A) golf
B) volleyball
C) dodge ball

GRADE 5 QUESTION

BIOLOGY

GRADE 1 QUESTION

True or false? All adult kangaroos have pouches.

ASTRONOMY

What constellation contains the Big Dipper?

GRADE 4 QUESTION

BIOLOGY

True or false? Chickens are cold-blooded animals.

GRADE 2 QUESTION

MATH

What is the only prime number that is a factor of 16?

GRADE 5 QUESTION

MEASUREMENT

What unit of power is abbreviated by the letter W?

GRADE 3 QUESTION

GRADE 1 QUESTION

WORLD HISTORY

True or false? The year 1616 was in the 17th century.

QUIZ 9

ENGLISH

What is the root word in the word "longest"?

GRADE 1 QUESTION

MUSIC

True or false? By definition, all operas are sung in Italian.

GRADE 3 QUESTION

SCIENCE

Lightning is what type of electricity?
A) current
B) alternating
C) static

GRADE 4 QUESTION

SPELLING

The names of how many months of the year contain the letter R?

GRADE 2 QUESTION

U.S. HISTORY

Who was the first U.S. Secretary of the Treasury?

GRADE 5 QUESTION

QUIZ 10

GRADE 4 QUESTION

MATH

What is the product of 2/3 and 48?

GRADE 3 QUESTION

ANIMAL SCIENCE

True or false? The orca is a type of dolphin.

GRADE 1 QUESTION

U.S. STUDIES

What U.S. state is nicknamed the Lone Star State?

GRADE 2 QUESTION

GEOGRAPHY

What city is the capital of Japan?

GRADE 5 QUESTION

LITERATURE

What 19th-century British author wrote the novel *Oliver Twist*?

QUIZ 11

MATH

Which number has a 7 in the tens place?
A) 75   B) 57   C) 157

GRADE 1 QUESTION

SCIENCE

True or false?
Adding salt to water lowers its freezing point.

GRADE 3 QUESTION

MEASUREMENT

How many feet are in a mile?

GRADE 2 QUESTION

GEOGRAPHY

Which of the Great Lakes lies farthest east?

GRADE 5 QUESTION

U.S. HISTORY

In what year was Abraham Lincoln first elected U.S. President?

GRADE 4 QUESTION

QUIZ 12

MATH

What is 309 rounded to the nearest hundred?

GRADE 2 QUESTION

U.S. HISTORY

True or false? Paul Revere participated in the Boston Tea Party.

GRADE 3 QUESTION

GEOGRAPHY

The U.S. state of Hawaii is located in which ocean?

GRADE 1 QUESTION

MEASUREMENT

How many pecks equal one bushel?

GRADE 5 QUESTION

ENGLISH

What is the infinitive of the verb "went"?

GRADE 4 QUESTION

QUIZ 13

BIOLOGY

What is the largest animal on earth?

ASTRONOMY

The planet Earth is located in what galaxy?

MATH

What is the reciprocal of 3/4?

U.S. STUDIES

What state's nickname is the Show Me State?

EARTH SCIENCE

By definition, an anemometer measures the speed of what?

QUIZ 14

GEOGRAPHY

What is the capital of Thailand?

GRADE 3 QUESTION

ANIMAL SCIENCE

True or false? The koala is a marsupial.

GRADE 1 QUESTION

U.S. HISTORY

What famous American was born on February 22, 1732?

GRADE 2 QUESTION

MEASUREMENT

One gallon equals how many pints?

GRADE 4 QUESTION

ANATOMY

Which are blood vessels in the human body?
A) tibias
B) cilia
C) capillaries

GRADE 5 QUESTION

WHAT STARS IS CLOSET TO EARTH?

QUIZ 15

GRADE QUESTION 1

MATH

A rectangle has how many sides?

GRADE QUESTION 3

ASTRONOMY

True or false? The Milky Way galaxy contains more than one billion stars.

GRADE QUESTION 2

ANIMAL SCIENCE

What living bird lays the biggest eggs?

GRADE QUESTION 4

GEOGRAPHY

In terms of area, what is the largest desert in Africa?

GRADE QUESTION 5

LITERATURE

Gulliver's Travels was written by what 18th-century author?

MEASUREMENT

How many cups are in five and a half gallons?

GRADE 4 QUESTION

SCIENCE

Which element comprises the majority of Earth's atmosphere?

GRADE 5 QUESTION

ASTRONOMY

What is the only planet in our solar system that man has walked on?

GRADE 1 QUESTION

GEOGRAPHY

After China, what country has the biggest population?

GRADE 2 QUESTION

MATH

An isosceles triangle has how many equal sides?

GRADE 3 QUESTION

ENGLISH

What is the prefix of the word "unfortunately"?

GRADE 2 QUESTION

U.S. HISTORY

Who was the only person to be elected U.S. President four times?

GRADE 5 QUESTION

SCIENCE

Famous scientist Albert Einstein was born in what country?

GRADE 4 QUESTION

MATH

How many degrees are in a quarter of a circle?

GRADE 3 QUESTION

MEASUREMENT

How many seconds are in half a minute?

GRADE 1 QUESTION

ANIMAL SCIENCE

A giant panda's natural habitat is on what continent?

EARTH SCIENCE

In the Northern Hemisphere, summer ends in which month?

MATH

If $y = 3x$, and $3x = 12$, then what number does y equal?

GOVERNMENT

How long is one regular term for a U.S. Senator?

LITERATURE

The Little Mermaid was written by what 19th-century author?

QUIZ 19

GRADE 1 QUESTION

GEOGRAPHY

Which ocean borders the U.S. state of Georgia?

GRADE 2 QUESTION

HEALTH

Typical people have how many baby teeth as kids?
A) 20   B) 24   C) 28

GRADE 5 QUESTION

MATH

Any number to the power of zero
is equal to what value?

U.S. HISTORY

What is the first
name of former U.S.
President Taylor?

GRADE 4 QUESTION

ANIMAL SCIENCE

True or false?
Only male lions
have manes.

GRADE 3 QUESTION

QUIZ 20

GEOGRAPHY

Mount Kilimanjaro is located on what continent?

ANIMAL SCIENCE

The female of what animal is called a ewe?

CULTURAL STUDIES

What modern holiday is also known as All Hallows' Eve?

ASTRONOMY

The planet Mars has how many moons?

MEASUREMENT

How many teaspoons are in five tablespoons?

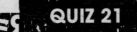

QUIZ 21

U.S. HISTORY

Who was the first Chief Justice of the U.S. Supreme Court?

GRADE 5 QUESTION

ANATOMY

GRADE 2 QUESTION

True or false?
The small intestine is longer than the large intestine.

EARTH SCIENCE

In the Southern Hemisphere, the vernal equinox occurs in which month?

ENGLISH

An example of an oxymoron is:
A) peanut gallery
B) rhyme time
C) living dead

GRADE 4 QUESTION

GRADE 3 QUESTION

GOVERNMENT

GRADE 1 QUESTION

True or false? The President and Vice President live in the White House.

ANIMAL SCIENCE

True or false?
Walruses are native
to the Arctic.

GRADE 1 QUESTION

MATH

True or false?
8/7 is an
improper
fraction.

GRADE 2 QUESTION

SOCIAL STUDIES

The United Nations headquarters are in what city?

GRADE 3 QUESTION

GEOGRAPHY

The names of
how many U.S.
states begin with
the letter O?

GRADE 4 QUESTION

GRAMMAR

GRADE 5 QUESTION

How many nouns
are in: Jake likes
swimming in the
wide lake.

WHAT STARTS
CLOSET TO EARTH?

QUIZ 23

CULTURAL STUDIES

Buddhism is a religion that began in what country?

GRADE 4 QUESTION

GEOGRAPHY

In terms of land area, what is the smallest state?

GRADE 1 QUESTION

MEASUREMENT

How many meters are in a kilometer?

GRADE 2 QUESTION

ANATOMY

True or false? The kidneys are part of the human digestive system.

GRADE 3 QUESTION

MATH

What is the product of 1.1 and 1.1?

GRADE 5 QUESTION

GEOGRAPHY

Russia's longest land border is with what other country?

GRADE 5 QUESTION

MATH

How many sides are there on a trapezoid?

GRADE 4 QUESTION

GRADE 1 QUESTION

SCIENCE

True or false? A spider is an insect.

U.S. STUDIES

What is the capital of Massachusetts?

GRADE 3 QUESTION

GRAMMAR

What is the verb in: It is such a nice day!

GRADE 2 QUESTION

QUIZ 25

GEOGRAPHY

True or false?
North America is in the
Eastern Hemisphere.

GRADE 3 QUESTION

SCIENCE

Which of the
following trees is
considered a
conifer?
A) oak
B) pine
C) maple

GRADE 4 QUESTION

HEALTH

What Scottish
scientist discovered
penicillin in 1928?

GRADE 5 QUESTION

MATH

True or false?
The sum of two
odd numbers
will always be
an even
number.

GRADE 1 QUESTION

ANATOMY

The typical human has
how many lungs?

GRADE 2 QUESTION

U.S. STUDIES

GRADE 1 QUESTION

In what U.S. state is the Lincoln Home National Historic Site?

EARTH SCIENCE

GRADE 2 QUESTION

True or false? A river's place of origin is its mouth.

GEOGRAPHY

What is the capital of the United Kingdom?

GRADE 3 QUESTION

MEASUREMENT

GRADE 4 QUESTION

How many ounces are in one gallon?

ANATOMY

What organ in the human body produces insulin?

GRADE 5 QUESTION

QUIZ 27

MEASUREMENT

GRADE 5 QUESTION

How many watts are used during one kilowatt-hour?

SPELLING

GRADE 1 QUESTION

The name of which day of the week comes last alphabetically?

MATH

GRADE 3 QUESTION

What is the range of the numbers 8, 3, 7, and 6?

ANIMAL SCIENCE

GRADE 2 QUESTION

Which of the following is a venomous snake?
A) python
B) cobra
C) anaconda

GEOGRAPHY

GRADE 4 QUESTION

Ivan the Terrible was a czar of what country?

QUIZ 28

MATH

What is the product of 4/5 and 125?

GRADE 4 QUESTION

MUSIC

The two most common clefs used in modern music are the treble and what other clef?

GRADE 5 QUESTION

SPELLING

What month comes last alphabetically?

GRADE 2 QUESTION

ANIMAL SCIENCE

True or false? The Alaskan malamute is a species of fish.

GRADE 3 QUESTION

GRADE 1 QUESTION

ENGLISH

How many apostrophes are missing from: Nathans dog licked its paw.

GRADE 5 QUESTION

U.S. HISTORY

Who was the only U.S. President who never married?

GEOGRAPHY

How many U.S. states border the Pacific Ocean?

GRADE 2 QUESTION

MATH

What number is 11 more than 55 and 9 less than 75?

SCIENCE

What scientist developed the equation $E = mc^2$?

GRADE 1 QUESTION

GRADE 4 QUESTION

GRADE 3 QUESTION

ENGLISH

What is the singular form of the word lice?

U.S. HISTORY

In 1782, what became the official bird of the United States?

ANIMAL SCIENCE

How many arms does a typical octopus have?

GRADE QUESTION 1

GRADE QUESTION 2

MEASUREMENT

If Cody's baby sister weighs 8 pounds, how many ounces does she weigh?

GRADE QUESTION 3

GEOGRAPHY

Bern is the capital of what European country?

MUSIC

What composer wrote the *1812 Overture* in 1882?

GRADE QUESTION 4

GRADE QUESTION 5

WORLD HISTORY

True or false?
Vikings, also known
as Norsemen,
originated in
Scandinavia.

MEASUREMENT

How many square
feet are in a three-
yard-square area?

GRADE 3 QUESTION

GRADE 5 QUESTION

MATH

The supplementary angle
of a 60-degree angle has
how many degrees?

GEOGRAPHY

The U.S. state
of Indiana
borders which
Great Lake?

GRADE 4 QUESTION

GRADE 1 QUESTION

GRADE 2 QUESTION

EARTH SCIENCE

True or false? Plants are not part of the food chain.

AaBbCcD

7x=49

HEALTH

How many canine teeth are in a typical adult human mouth?

GRADE 4 QUESTION

ANIMAL SCIENCE

True or false? The wolverine is a member of the canine family.

GRADE 2 QUESTION

AT STAR IS
LOSET TO EAR

x y

6yz

GRADE 5 QUESTION

EARTH SCIENCE

Coal and diamonds are made of what element?

KANSAS

HIST

KENTUCKY

E

MEASUREMENT

Of the current U.S. coins, which is smallest in size?

P.E.

To the nearest mile, how long is a standard Olympic marathon?

GRADE 1 QUESTION

GRADE 3 QUESTION

A B

MATH

What whole number is the closest to the square root of 50?

GRADE 4 QUESTION

GEOGRAPHY

Yosemite National Park is located in what U.S. state?

GRADE 2 QUESTION

BIOLOGY

A typical amoeba has how many cells?

GRADE 3 QUESTION

ASTRONOMY

What was the name of the first American woman to travel into outer space?

GRADE 5 QUESTION

EARTH SCIENCE

True or false? Lightning is a form of precipitation.

GRADE 1 QUESTION

QUIZ 34

U.S. STUDIES

How many U.S. states have the word North, South, East, or West in their names?

GRADE 2 QUESTION

MEASUREMENT

In the U.S., how many pounds are in a ton?

GRADE 5 QUESTION

GEOGRAPHY

What is the capital of Brazil?

GRADE 4 QUESTION

MATH

At 48 cents a pound, how much does 5/8 of a pound of peanuts cost?

GRADE 3 QUESTION

LITERATURE

In folklore, what is the name of Paul Bunyan's blue ox?

GRADE 1 QUESTION

U.S. STUDIES

GRADE 5 QUESTION

Two U.S. states were formed during the Civil War: Nevada and which other?

MATH

GRADE 4 QUESTION

How many factors does the number 121 have?

EARTH SCIENCE

GRADE 3 QUESTION

True or false? Cocoa beans, from which chocolate is made, originated in Asia.

GRADE 1 QUESTION

MUSIC

Timpani are members of what musical family?

GEOGRAPHY

U.S. Studies
In terms of land area, what is the second-biggest U.S. state?

GRADE 2 QUESTION

QUIZ 36

MATH

What is the absolute value of 9?

GRADE 5 QUESTION

MUSIC

True or false?
A beat with no sound is called a rest.

GRADE 1 QUESTION

GEOGRAPHY

Sweden's longest land border is with what other country?

GRADE 4 QUESTION

SCIENCE

What state of matter is ice?
A) solid
B) gas
C) liquid

GRADE 2 QUESTION

ART

On the color wheel, what color is complementary to orange?

GRADE 3 QUESTION

MATH

True or false? The sum of the digits in the number 768 is equal to 22.

GRADE 1 QUESTION

CHEMISTRY

What is the lightest noble gas?

GRADE 5 QUESTION

ENGLISH

"Wept" is the past tense form of what verb?

GRADE 3 QUESTION

GEOGRAPHY

The Allegheny and Monongahela rivers meet and form the Ohio River in what U.S. city?

GRADE 4 QUESTION

SPELLING

The plural form of the word "quiz" has how many letters?

GRADE 2 QUESTION

BIOLOGY

What gas do humans exhale that plants need to live?

U.S. STUDIES

Which U.S. President is featured on the face of the nickel?

GRADE QUESTION 2

ANIMAL SCIENCE

In terms of average size, what is the largest species of penguin?

GRADE QUESTION 3

MATH

What is the least common multiple of 6 and 10?

GRADE QUESTION 4

WORLD HISTORY

Who became the first chairman of the People's Republic of China in 1949?

GRADE QUESTION 5

WHAT STAR IS CLOSET TO EARTH?

QUIZ 39

SCIENCE

How many horns did *Triceratops* have on its head?

GRADE 1 QUESTION

GEOGRAPHY

Which continent is the least populated?

GRADE 2 QUESTION

CULTURAL STUDIES

In Greek mythology, who was the father of Apollo?

GRADE 4 QUESTION

MATH

What is the area of a square that has a 24cm perimeter?

GRADE 5 QUESTION

U.S. HISTORY

In what U.S. state was the Civil War Battle of Gettysburg fought?

GRADE 3 QUESTION

AaBb

BIOLOGY

An animal without a backbone is an:
A) invertebrate
B) anthropoid
C) amphibian

GRADE 3 QUESTION

U.S. HISTORY

What U.S. President only served one month in office?

GRADE 5 QUESTION

LITERATURE

In Homer's *Odyssey*, the monster Cyclops has how many eyes?

GRADE 4 QUESTION

KANSAS
KENTUCKY

HIST

CULTURAL STUDIES

The holiday Cinco de Mayo originated in what country?

ASTRONOMY

How many confirmed planets (as of October 2016) are in our solar system?

GRADE 1 QUESTION

GRADE 2 QUESTION

QUIZ 41

ANIMAL SCIENCE

True or false? Komodo dragons are extinct.

GRADE 1 QUESTION

U.S. STUDIES

The U.S. Naval Academy is located in what city?

GRADE 4 QUESTION

MATH

What is the sum of the degrees of the interior angles of an octagon?

GRADE 5 QUESTION

GEOGRAPHY

France borders which ocean?

GRADE 2 QUESTION

ENGLISH

What part of speech is the first word in: How do you do?

GRADE 3 QUESTION

QUIZ 42

GEOGRAPHY

The headwaters of the Mississippi River are in what U.S. state?

MATH

If 15/35 = n/7, then *n* must be equal to what number?

ANIMAL SCIENCE

Which is not a fish:
A) manta ray   B) porpoise   C) sea horse

GRAMMAR

How many nouns are in this question?

U.S. HISTORY

True or false? Betsy Ross was a U.S. First Lady.

GEOGRAPHY

GRADE 5 QUESTION

Timbuktu is a city in what African country?

ANIMAL SCIENCE

GRADE 1 QUESTION

True or false? A camel's hump is primarily used to hold water.

ASTRONOMY

GRADE 3 QUESTION

True or false? The sun is the only star in our solar system.

ENGLISH

GRADE 4 QUESTION

MATH

What is the greatest common factor of 12 and 36?

ENGLISH

GRADE 2 QUESTION

True or false? The word "true" is an antonym of the word "false."

AaBbCcDdEe

QUIZ 44

MATH

GRADE 4 QUESTION

What is the numeric value of the Roman numeral L?

GEOGRAPHY

GRADE 2 QUESTION

Active volcano Mount St. Helens is in what U.S. state?

ANIMAL SCIENCE

GRADE 5 QUESTION

The octopus belongs to what class of animals?

GRAMMAR

GRADE 1 QUESTION

What is the adjective in: Olivia has ten fingers on which to count numbers.

PHYSICS

GRADE 3 QUESTION

A lever is a simple machine that pivots on a point called a: A) fulcrum   B) levee   C) pulley

GRADE 4 QUESTION

SPELLING

Which of the following words is spelled incorrectly?
A) privilege B) villege C) appendage

GEOGRAPHY

What is the world's longest river?

GRADE 3 QUESTION

ANIMAL SCIENCE

True or false?
Some species of
sea turtles live in
freshwater lakes.

GRADE 1 QUESTION

MATH

How many faces are
there on a cube?

GRADE 2 QUESTION

GRADE 5 QUESTION

WORLD HISTORY

Who is the longest-reigning British monarch?

QUIZ 46

GRAMMAR

The word "you" is what type of pronoun?
A) first person
B) second person
C) third person

GRADE 3 QUESTION

U.S. HISTORY

What was the first name of U.S. President Hayes, elected into office in 1876?

GRADE 4 QUESTION

GEOGRAPHY

True or false? There are no glaciers in Africa.

GRADE 2 QUESTION

ANIMAL SCIENCE

True or false? Roadrunners are birds.

GRADE 1 QUESTION

MATH

What's the volume (in cm^3) of a cube with surface area of 96 cm^2 ?

GRADE 5 QUESTION

QUIZ 47

GRAMMAR

Which of the following is NOT an article?
A) an
B) the
C) to

GRADE 2 QUESTION

GEOGRAPHY

Copenhagen is the capital of what European country?

GRADE 4 QUESTION

MATH

What is the sum of all the even numbers between 1 and 9?

GRADE 1 QUESTION

BIOLOGY

What is NOT part of an animal cell?
A) ribosome
B) chloroplast
C) cytoplasm

GRADE 5 QUESTION

EARTH SCIENCE

In order for iron to rust, it needs to be exposed to both water and what gaseous element?

GRADE 3 QUESTION

7x7=49   AaBbCcDdE

ENGLISH

"Won't" is a contraction of what two words?

GRADE
QUESTION
1

GEOGRAPHY

Which of the following states extends the farthest north?
A) Wyoming
B) Idaho
C) Utah

GRADE
QUESTION
2

WHAT STAR IS
LOSET TO EAR   x y

U.S. HISTORY

Who was President of the U.S. in 1800?

GRADE
QUESTION
4

KANSAS   HIST
KENTUCKY   EN

MEASUREMENT

How many cups are in 5 U.S. liquid quarts?

ANIMAL SCIENCE

True or false? All arthropods are invertebrates

GRADE
QUESTION
5

GRADE
QUESTION
3

A B

DID YOU MAKE THE GRADE?

To find out, all you need to do is add up your score.

Each quiz has a question for each Grade level: 1, 2, 3, 4, 5

For each correct answer, you score:
Grade 1, 1 point
Grade 2, 2 points
Grade 3, 3 points
Grade 4, 4 points
Grade 5, 5 points

A perfect score for each quiz is 15 points.

15, 14, or 13 points—You're an A+ student!
12, 11, 10 points—Not bad! Congrats!
9, 8, 7, 6 points—That's okay. Just keep pluggin'!
5 and below—Next quiz will be better!

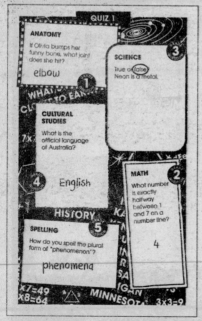

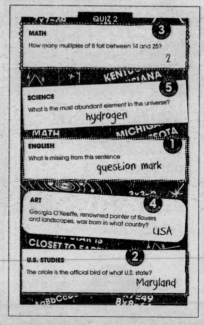

Your Score: **Your Score:**

ANSWERS

QUIZ 3

MUSIC
True or false? A cello is larger in size than a viola. (True circled)

ENGLISH
What is the preposition in:
Man has walked on the moon.   on

CULTURAL STUDIES
The Nobel Peace Prize is presented annually in what country?   Norway

ANATOMY
True or false?
The human shoulder is a ball-and-socket joint. (True circled)

ENGLISH

SCIENCE
True or false?
Salt is a mineral. (True circled)

Your Score:

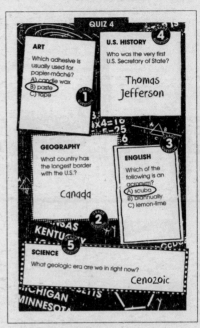

QUIZ 4

ART
Which adhesive is usually used for papier-mâché?
A) candle wax
B) paste (circled)
C) tape

U.S. HISTORY
Who was the very first U.S. Secretary of State?   Thomas Jefferson

GEOGRAPHY
What country has the longest border with the U.S.?   Canada

ENGLISH
Which of the following is an acronym?
A) scuba (circled)
B) biannually
C) lemon-lime

SCIENCE
What geologic era are we in right now?   Cenozoic

Your Score:

QUIZ 5

ANIMAL SCIENCE
What is the heaviest land animal?   elephant

GEOGRAPHY
What is the capital of Sweden?   Stockholm

MATH
How many sides does a rhombus have?   4

MEASUREMENT
How many decades are in two millennia?   200

U.S. HISTORY
Who was the first U.S. President to be impeached?   Andrew Johnson

Your Score:

QUIZ 6

GEOGRAPHY
What is the only continent that is also a country?   Australia

LITERATURE
Who wrote the book *Little House on the Prairie*?   Laura Ingalls Wilder

U.S. HISTORY
True or false? Benjamin Franklin served as a senator from Pennsylvania. (false circled)

ASTRONOMY
True or false?
The planet Jupiter has a larger mass than Earth. (True circled)

ANATOMY
How many incisors are there in a typical adult human mouth?   8

Your Score:

ANSWERS

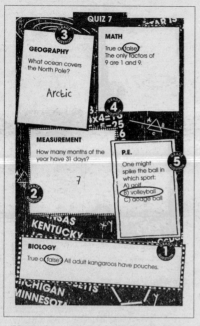

QUIZ 7

GEOGRAPHY
What ocean covers the North Pole?

Arctic

MATH
True or (false)?
The only factors of 9 are 1 and 9.

MEASUREMENT
How many months of the year have 31 days?

7

P.E.
One might spike the ball in which sport:
A) golf
B) volleyball
C) dodge ball

BIOLOGY
True or (false)? All adult kangaroos have pouches.

Your Score:

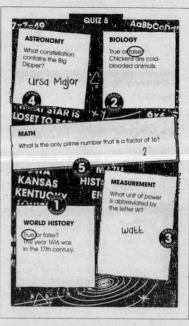

QUIZ 8

ASTRONOMY
What constellation contains the Big Dipper?

Ursa Major

BIOLOGY
True or (false)?
Chickens are cold-blooded animals.

MATH
What is the only prime number that is a factor of 16?

2

MEASUREMENT
What unit of power is abbreviated by the letter W?

watt

WORLD HISTORY
(True) or false?
The year 1616 was in the 17th century.

Your Score:

QUIZ 9

ENGLISH
What is the root word in the word "longest"?

long

MUSIC
True or (false)?
By definition, all operas are sung in Italian.

SCIENCE
Lightning is what type of electricity?
A) current
B) alternating
C) static

SPELLING
The names of how many months of the year contain the letter R?

8

U.S. HISTORY
Who was the first U.S. Secretary of the Treasury?

Alexander Hamilton

Your Score:

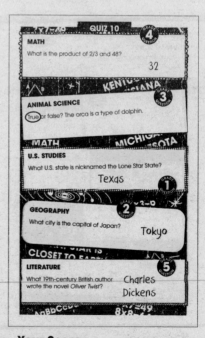

QUIZ 10

MATH
What is the product of 2/3 and 48?

32

ANIMAL SCIENCE
(True) or false? The orca is a type of dolphin.

U.S. STUDIES
What U.S. state is nicknamed the Lone Star State?

Texas

GEOGRAPHY
What city is the capital of Japan?

Tokyo

LITERATURE
What 19th-century British author wrote the novel *Oliver Twist*?

Charles Dickens

Your Score:

ANSWERS

QUIZ 11

MATH
Which number has a 7 in the tens place?
A) 75 B) 57 C) 157
(A) 75 circled
①

SCIENCE
True or false?
Adding salt to water lowers its freezing point.
(True circled)
③

MEASUREMENT
How many feet are in a mile?
5280
②

ENGLISH
④

U.S. HISTORY
In what year was Abraham Lincoln first elected U.S. President?
1860

GEOGRAPHY
Which of the Great Lakes lies farthest east?
Ontario
⑤

Your Score:

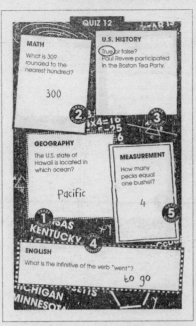

QUIZ 12

MATH
What is 309 rounded to the nearest hundred?
300
②

U.S. HISTORY
True or false?
Paul Revere participated in the Boston Tea Party.
(True circled)
③

GEOGRAPHY
The U.S. state of Hawaii is located in which ocean?
Pacific
①

MEASUREMENT
How many pecks equal one bushel?
4
⑤

ENGLISH
What is the infinitive of the verb "went"?
to go
④

Your Score:

QUIZ 13

BIOLOGY
What is the largest animal on earth?
blue whale
①

ASTRONOMY
The planet Earth is located in what galaxy?
Milky Way
②

MATH
What is the reciprocal of 3/4?
1 1/3
④

U.S. STUDIES
What state's nickname is the Show Me State?
Missouri
③

EARTH SCIENCE
By definition, an anemometer measures the speed of what?
wind speed
⑤

Your Score:

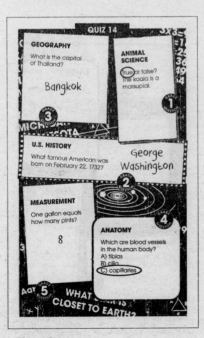

QUIZ 14

GEOGRAPHY
What is the capital of Thailand?
Bangkok
③

ANIMAL SCIENCE
True or false?
The koala is a marsupial.
(True circled)
①

U.S. HISTORY
What famous American was born on February 22, 1732?
George Washington
②

MEASUREMENT
One gallon equals how many pints?
8
⑤

ANATOMY
Which are blood vessels in the human body?
A) tibias
B) cilia
C) capillaries
(C) capillaries circled)
④

Your Score:

ANSWERS

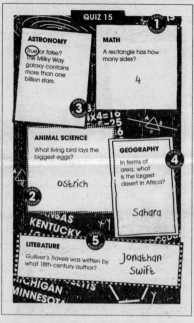

QUIZ 15

ASTRONOMY
True or false? The Milky Way galaxy contains more than one billion stars.

MATH
A rectangle has how many sides?

4

ANIMAL SCIENCE
What living bird lays the biggest eggs?

ostrich

GEOGRAPHY
In terms of area, what is the largest desert in Africa?

Sahara

LITERATURE
Gulliver's Travels was written by what 18th-century author?

Jonathan Swift

Your Score:

QUIZ 16

MEASUREMENT
How many cups are in five and a half gallons?

88

SCIENCE
Which element comprises the majority of Earth's atmosphere?

nitrogen

ASTRONOMY
What is the only planet in our solar system that man has walked on?

Earth

GEOGRAPHY
After China, what country has the biggest population?

India

MATH
An isosceles triangle has how many equal sides?

2

Your Score:

QUIZ 17

ENGLISH
What is the prefix of the word "unfortunately"?

un-

U.S. HISTORY
Who was the only person to be elected U.S. President four times?

Franklin Roosevelt

SCIENCE
Famous scientist Albert Einstein was born in what country?

Germany

MATH
How many degrees are in a quarter of a circle?

90

MEASUREMENT
How many seconds are in half a minute?

30

Your Score:

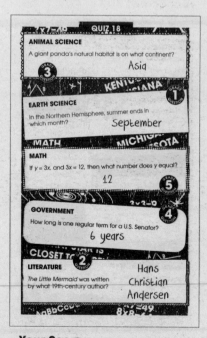

QUIZ 18

ANIMAL SCIENCE
A giant panda's natural habitat is on what continent?

Asia

EARTH SCIENCE
In the Northern Hemisphere, summer ends in which month?

September

MATH
If $y = 3x$, and $3x = 12$, then what number does y equal?

12

GOVERNMENT
How long is one regular term for a U.S. Senator?

6 years

LITERATURE
The Little Mermaid was written by what 19th-century author?

Hans Christian Andersen

Your Score:

ANSWERS

QUIZ 19

GEOGRAPHY
Which ocean borders the U.S. state of Georgia?
Atlantic

HEALTH
Typical people have how many baby teeth as kids?
A) 20 B) 24 C) 28

MATH
Any number to the power of zero is equal to what value?
1

ANIMAL SCIENCE
True or false? Only male lions have manes.

U.S. HISTORY
What is the first name of former U.S. President Taylor?
Zachary

Your Score:

QUIZ 20

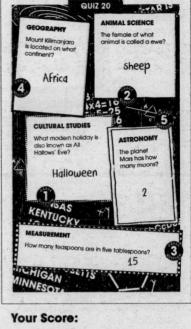

GEOGRAPHY
Mount Kilimanjaro is located on what continent?
Africa

ANIMAL SCIENCE
The female of what animal is called a ewe?
sheep

CULTURAL STUDIES
What modern holiday is also known as All Hallows' Eve?
Halloween

ASTRONOMY
The planet Mars has how many moons?
2

MEASUREMENT
How many teaspoons are in five tablespoons?
15

Your Score:

QUIZ 21

U.S. HISTORY
Who was the first Chief Justice of the U.S. Supreme Court?
John Jay

ANATOMY
True or false? The small intestine is longer than the large intestine.

EARTH SCIENCE
In the Southern Hemisphere, the vernal equinox occurs in which month?
September

ENGLISH
An example of an oxymoron is:
A) peanut gallery
B) rhyme time
C) living dead

GOVERNMENT
True or false? The President and Vice President live in the White House.

Your Score:

QUIZ 22

ANIMAL SCIENCE
True or false? Walruses are native to the Arctic.

MATH
True or false? 8/7 is an improper fraction.

SOCIAL STUDIES
The United Nations headquarters are in what city?
New York City

GEOGRAPHY
The names of how many U.S. states begin with the letter O?
3

GRAMMAR
How many nouns are in: Jake likes swimming in the wide lake.
3

Your Score:

ANSWERS

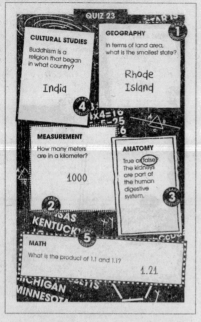

QUIZ 23

CULTURAL STUDIES
Buddhism is a religion that began in what country?

India

GEOGRAPHY
In terms of land area, what is the smallest state?

Rhode Island

MEASUREMENT
How many meters are in a kilometer?

1000

ANATOMY
True or false? The kidneys are part of the human digestive system.

MATH
What is the product of 1.1 and 1.1?

1.21

Your Score:

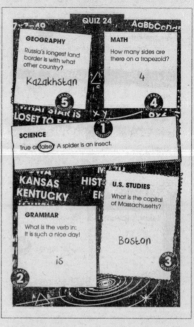

QUIZ 24

GEOGRAPHY
Russia's longest land border is with what other country?

Kazakhstan

MATH
How many sides are there on a trapezoid?

4

SCIENCE
True or *false*? A spider is an insect.

GRAMMAR
What is the verb in: It is such a nice day!

is

U.S. STUDIES
What is the capital of Massachusetts?

Boston

Your Score:

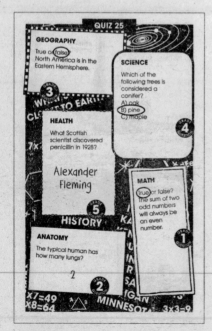

QUIZ 25

GEOGRAPHY
True or *false*? North America is in the Eastern Hemisphere.

SCIENCE
Which of the following trees is considered a conifer?
A) oak
B) pine
C) maple

HEALTH
What Scottish scientist discovered penicillin in 1928?

Alexander Fleming

MATH
True or false? The sum of two odd numbers will always be an even number.

ANATOMY
The typical human has how many lungs?

2

Your Score:

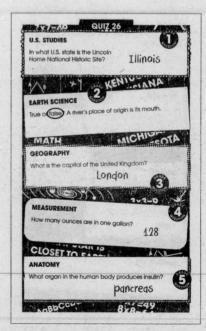

QUIZ 26

U.S. STUDIES
In what U.S. state is the Lincoln Home National Historic Site?

Illinois

EARTH SCIENCE
True or *false*? A river's place of origin is its mouth.

GEOGRAPHY
What is the capital of the United Kingdom?

London

MEASUREMENT
How many ounces are in one gallon?

128

ANATOMY
What organ in the human body produces insulin?

pancreas

Your Score:

ANSWERS

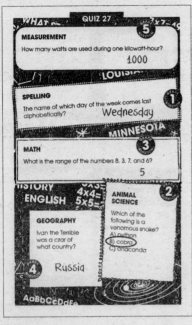

QUIZ 27

MEASUREMENT
How many watts are used during one kilowatt-hour?
1000

SPELLING
The name of which day of the week comes last alphabetically?
Wednesday

MATH
What is the range of the numbers 8, 3, 7, and 6?
5

GEOGRAPHY
Ivan the Terrible was a czar of what country?
Russia

ENGLISH

ANIMAL SCIENCE
Which of the following is a venomous snake?
A) python
B) cobra
C) anaconda

Your Score:

QUIZ 28

MATH
What is the product of 4/5 and 125?
100

MUSIC
The two most common clefs used in modern music are the treble and what other clef?
bass

SPELLING
What month comes last alphabetically?
september

ANIMAL SCIENCE
True or false: The Alaskan malamute is a species of fish.

ENGLISH
How many apostrophes are missing from: Nathans dog licked its paw.
one

Your Score:

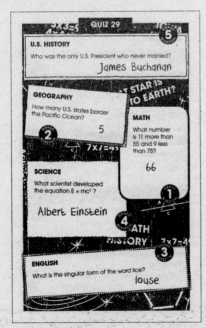

QUIZ 29

U.S. HISTORY
Who was the only U.S. President who never married?
James Buchanan

GEOGRAPHY
How many U.S. states border the Pacific Ocean?
5

MATH
What number is 11 more than 55 and 9 less than 75?
66

SCIENCE
What scientist developed the equation $E = mc^2$?
Albert Einstein

ENGLISH
What is the singular form of the word lice?
louse

Your Score:

QUIZ 30

U.S. HISTORY
In 1782, what became the official bird of the United States?
(bald) eagle

ANIMAL SCIENCE
How many arms does a typical octopus have?
8

MEASUREMENT
If Cody's baby sister weighs 8 pounds, how many ounces does she weigh?
128

GEOGRAPHY
Bern is the capital of what European country?
Switzerland

MUSIC
What composer wrote the 1812 Overture in 1882?
(Pyotr Ilyich) Tchaikovsky

Your Score:

ANSWERS

QUIZ 31

WORLD HISTORY
(True) or false?
Vikings, also known
as Norsemen,
originated in
Scandinavia.

③

MEASUREMENT
How many square
feet are in a three-
yard-square area?

81

⑤

MATH
The supplementary angle
of a 60-degree angle has
how many degrees?

120 degrees

④

GEOGRAPHY
The U.S. state
of Indiana
borders which
Great Lake?

Lake
Michigan

①

②

EARTH SCIENCE
True or (false?) Plants are not part of the food chain.

Your Score:

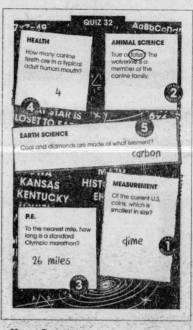

QUIZ 32

HEALTH
How many canine
teeth are in a typical
adult human mouth?

4

④

ANIMAL SCIENCE
True or (false?) The
wolverine is a
member of the
canine family.

②

⑤

EARTH SCIENCE
Coal and diamonds are made of what element?

carbon

KANSAS
KENTUCKY

P.E.
To the nearest mile, how
long is a standard
Olympic marathon?

26 miles

③

MEASUREMENT
Of the current U.S.
coins, which is
smallest in size?

dime

①

Your Score:

QUIZ 33

MATH
What whole number
is the closest to the
square root of 50?

7

④

GEOGRAPHY
Yosemite National Park
is located in what U.S.
state?

California

②

BIOLOGY
A typical amoeba
has how many
cells?

one

③

ASTRONOMY
What was the
name of the first
American
woman to travel
into outer
space?

⑤

Sally
Ride

①

EARTH SCIENCE
True or (false?) Lightning is a
form of precipitation.

Your Score:

QUIZ 34

U.S. STUDIES
How many U.S. states have the word North,
South, East, or West in their names?

5

②

⑤

MEASUREMENT
In the U.S., how many pounds are in a ton?

2000

MATH

GEOGRAPHY
What is the capital of Brazil?

Brasilia

④

MATH
At 48 cents a pound, how much does
5/8 of a pound of peanuts cost?

③

30 cents

LITERATURE
In folklore, what is the name of Paul Bunyan's blue ox?

Babe

①

Your Score:

ANSWERS

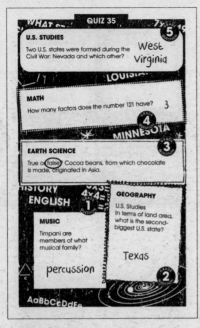

QUIZ 35

U.S. STUDIES
Two U.S. states were formed during the Civil War: Nevada and which other? — West Virginia

MATH
How many factors does the number 121 have? — 3

4

3

EARTH SCIENCE
True or (false): Cocoa beans, from which chocolate is made, originated in Asia.

MUSIC
Timpani are members of what musical family? — percussion

1

GEOGRAPHY
U.S. Studies
In terms of land area, what is the second-biggest U.S. state? — Texas

2

Your Score:

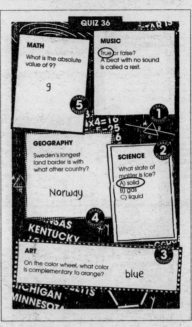

QUIZ 36

MATH
What is the absolute value of 9? — 9

MUSIC
(True) or false?
A beat with no sound is called a rest.

1

GEOGRAPHY
Sweden's longest land border is with what other country? — Norway

2

SCIENCE
What state of matter is ice?
A) solid
B) gas
C) liquid

3

ART
On the color wheel, what color is complementary to orange? — blue

Your Score:

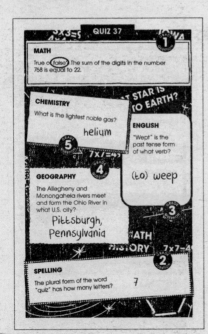

QUIZ 37

1

MATH
True or (false)? The sum of the digits in the number 768 is equal to 22.

CHEMISTRY
What is the lightest noble gas? — helium

5

ENGLISH
"Wept" is the past tense form of what verb? — (to) weep

4

GEOGRAPHY
The Allegheny and Monongahela rivers meet and form the Ohio River in what U.S. city? — Pittsburgh, Pennsylvania

3

2

SPELLING
The plural form of the word "quiz" has how many letters? — 7

Your Score:

QUIZ 38

BIOLOGY
What gas do humans exhale that plants need to live? — carbon dioxide

U.S. STUDIES
Which U.S. President is featured on the face of the nickel? — Thomas Jefferson

1

2

ANIMAL SCIENCE
In terms of average size, what is the largest species of penguin? — emperor

3

MATH
What is the least common multiple of 6 and 10? — 30

4

WORLD HISTORY
Who became the first chairman of the People's Republic of China in 1949? — Mao (Zedong)

5

Your Score:

ANSWERS

QUIZ 39

SCIENCE
How many horns did *Triceratops* have on its head?

3 ①

GEOGRAPHY
Which continent is the least populated?

Antarctica ②

CULTURAL STUDIES
In Greek mythology, who was the father of Apollo?

Zeus ④

MATH
What is the area of a square that has a 24cm perimeter?

36 cm ⑤

U.S. HISTORY
In what U.S. state was the Civil War Battle of Gettysburg fought?
Pennsylvania

Your Score:

QUIZ 40

BIOLOGY
An animal without a backbone is an:
A) invertebrate
B) arthropod
C) amphibian
③

U.S. HISTORY
What U.S. President only served one month in office?

William Harrison

LITERATURE
In Homer's *Odyssey*, the monster Cyclops has how many eyes?
one ④

CULTURAL STUDIES
The holiday Cinco de Mayo originated in what country?

Mexico

ASTRONOMY
How many confirmed planets (as of October 2016) are in our solar system?

8 ①

②

Your Score:

QUIZ 41

ANIMAL SCIENCE
True or false: Komodo dragons are extinct.
①

U.S. STUDIES
The U.S. Naval Academy is located in what city?

Annapolis, Maryland ④

MATH
What is the sum of the degrees of the interior angles of an octagon?

1080 ⑤

GEOGRAPHY
France borders which ocean?

Atlantic ②

ENGLISH
What part of speech is the first word in: How do you do?

adverb ③

Your Score:

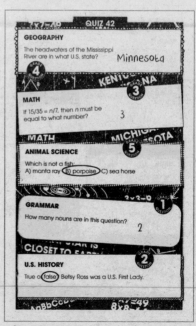

QUIZ 42

GEOGRAPHY
The headwaters of the Mississippi River are in what U.S. state? Minnesota
④

③

MATH
If 15/35 = *n*/7, then *n* must be equal to what number? 3

⑤

ANIMAL SCIENCE
Which is not a fish:
A) manta ray B) porpoise C) sea horse

GRAMMAR
How many nouns are in this question? 2
①

②

U.S. HISTORY
True or false: Betsy Ross was a U.S. First Lady.

Your Score:

ANSWERS

QUIZ 43

GEOGRAPHY ⑤
Timbuktu is a city in what African country?

Mali

ANIMAL SCIENCE ①
True or (false) A camel's hump is primarily used to hold water.

ASTRONOMY ③
(True) or false? The sun is the only star in our solar system.

ENGLISH ④

ENGLISH
(True) or false? The word "true" is an antonym of the word "false."

MATH
What is the greatest common factor of 12 and 36?

12 ②

Your Score:

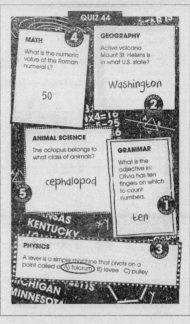

QUIZ 44

MATH ④
What is the numeric value of the Roman numeral L?

50

GEOGRAPHY ②
Active volcano Mount St. Helens is in what U.S. state?

Washington

ANIMAL SCIENCE ⑤
The octopus belongs to what class of animals?

cephalopod

GRAMMAR ①
What is the adjective in: Olivia has ten fingers on which to count numbers.

ten

PHYSICS ③
A lever is a simple machine that pivots on a point called a: (A) fulcrum B) levee C) pulley

Your Score:

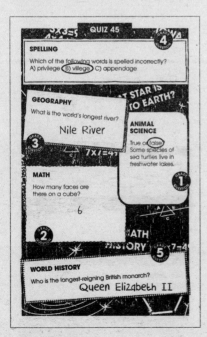

QUIZ 45

SPELLING ④
Which of the following words is spelled incorrectly?
A) privilege (B) villege C) appendage

GEOGRAPHY ③
What is the world's longest river?

Nile River

ANIMAL SCIENCE ①
True or (false)
Some species of sea turtles live in freshwater lakes.

MATH ②
How many faces are there on a cube?

6

WORLD HISTORY ⑤
Who is the longest-reigning British monarch?

Queen Elizabeth II

Your Score:

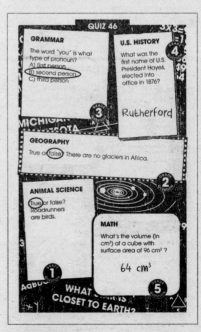

QUIZ 46

GRAMMAR ③
The word "you" is what type of pronoun?
A) first person
(B) second person
C) third person

U.S. HISTORY ④
What was the first name of U.S. President Hayes, elected into office in 1876?

Rutherford

GEOGRAPHY ②
True or (false) There are no glaciers in Africa.

ANIMAL SCIENCE ①
(True) or false?
Roadrunners are birds.

MATH ⑤
What's the volume (in cm^3) of a cube with surface area of 96 cm^2 ?

64 cm^3

Your Score:

ANSWERS

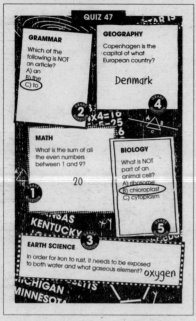

QUIZ 47

GRAMMAR
Which of the following is NOT an article?
A) an
B) the
C) to ⭕

GEOGRAPHY
Copenhagen is the capital of what European country?

Denmark

MATH
What is the sum of all the even numbers between 1 and 9?

20

BIOLOGY
What is NOT part of an animal cell?
A) ribosome
B) chloroplast ⭕
C) cytoplasm

EARTH SCIENCE
In order for iron to rust, it needs to be exposed to both water and what gaseous element? *oxygen*

Your Score:

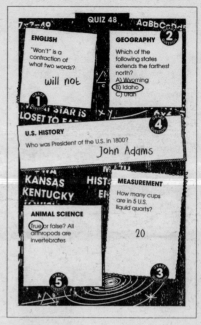

QUIZ 48

ENGLISH
"Won't" is a contraction of what two words?

will not

GEOGRAPHY
Which of the following states extends the farthest north?
A) Wyoming
B) Idaho ⭕
C) Utah

U.S. HISTORY
Who was President of the U.S. in 1800? *John Adams*

MEASUREMENT
How many cups are in 5 U.S. liquid quarts?

20

ANIMAL SCIENCE
True or false? All arthropods are invertebrates

Your Score: